I0813334

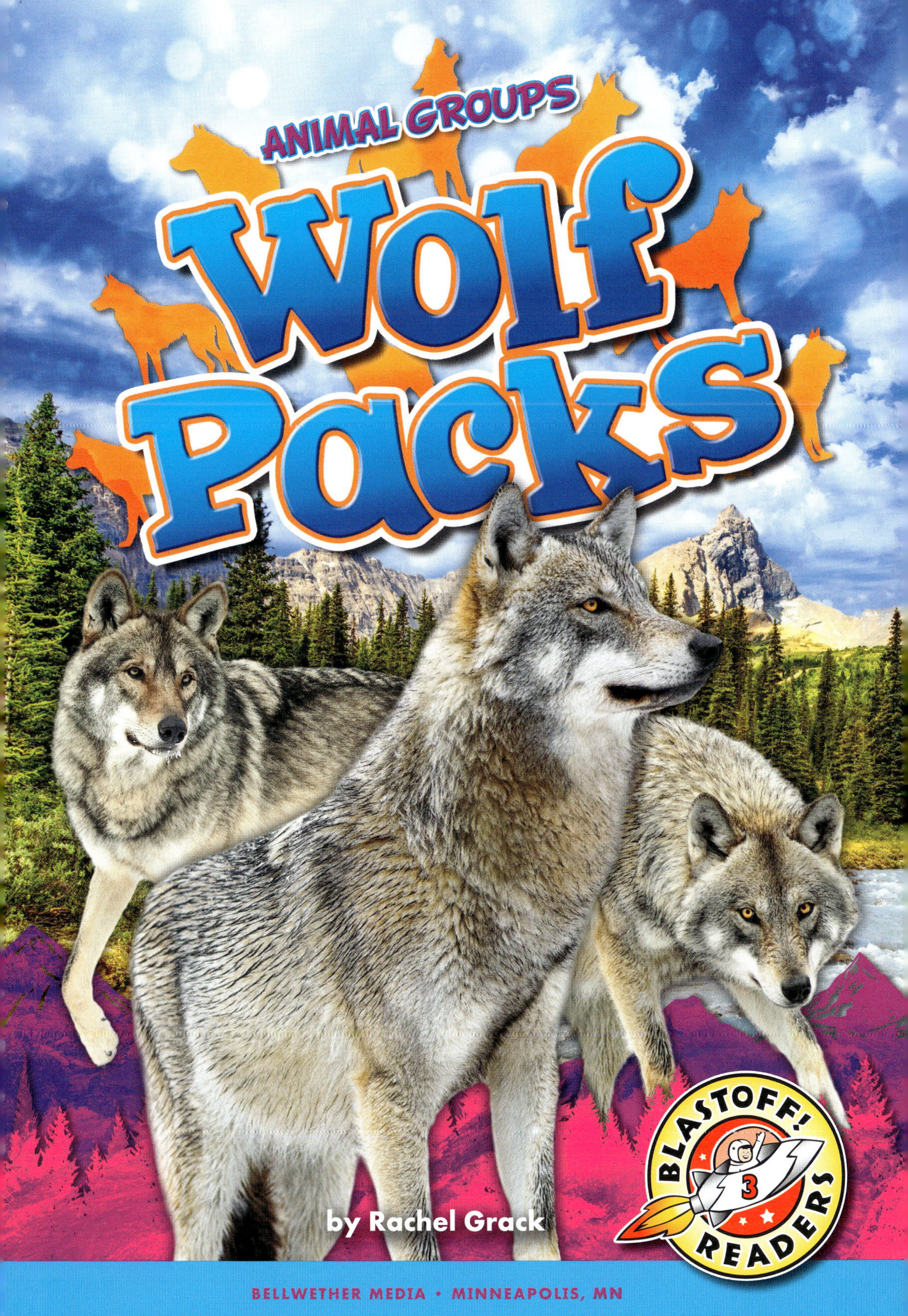
ANIMAL GROUPS
Wolf Packs
by Rachel Grack
BLASTOFF! 3 READERS
BELLWETHER MEDIA • MINNEAPOLIS, MN

**Blastoff! Readers** are carefully developed by literacy experts to build reading stamina and move students toward fluency by combining standards-based content with developmentally appropriate text.

**Level 1** provides the most support through repetition of high-frequency words, light text, predictable sentence patterns, and strong visual support.

**Level 2** offers early readers a bit more challenge through varied sentences, increased text load, and text-supportive special features.

**Level 3** advances early-fluent readers toward fluency through increased text load, less reliance on photos, advancing concepts, longer sentences, and more complex special features.

★ **Blastoff! Universe**

Reading Level

Grade K

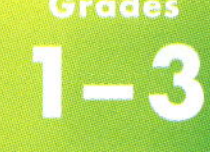

Grades 1–3

Grade 4

This edition first published in 2026 by Bellwether Media, Inc.



Library of Congress Cataloging-in-Publication Data

LC record for Wolf Packs available at: https://lccn.loc.gov/2025018603



Editor: Suzane Nguyen Designer: Brittany McIntosh

Printed in the United States of America, North Mankato, MN.

# Table of Contents


Wild Dogs 4
Pack Ranks 6
Hunting Team 12
Playful Pups 18
Glossary 22
To Learn More 23
Index 24

# Wild Dogs

Wolves are large wild dogs. Gray wolves are the most widespread. They live in forests, **grasslands**, and mountains.

Wolf packs can be found in North America, Europe, and Asia. They also live in parts of Africa.

# Pack Ranks

Packs have around 6 to 10 members. Most packs are made up of an **alpha pair** and their **offspring**.

Larger packs include uncles, aunts, and grandparents.

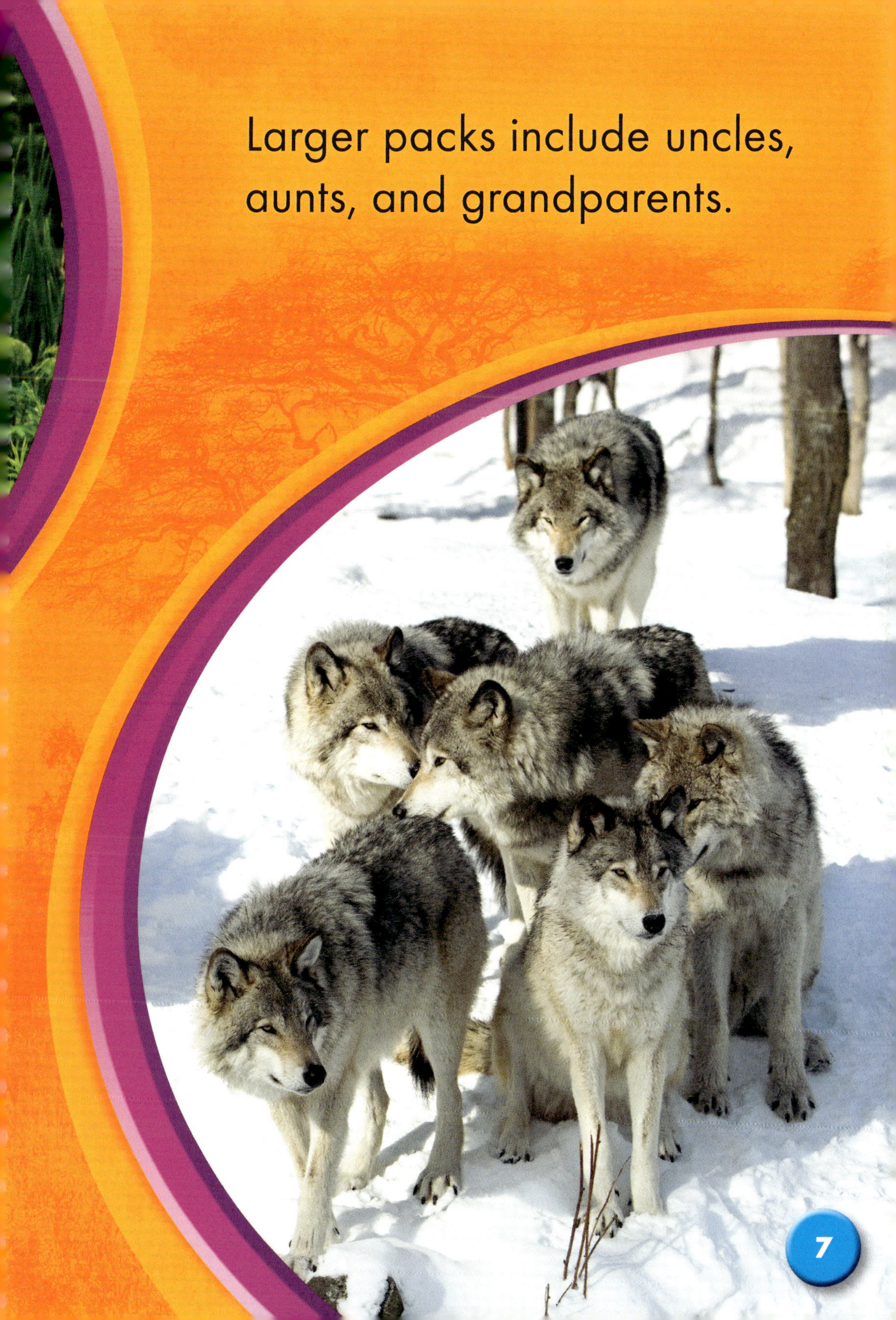

Pack members form strong **bonds**. The alpha pair leads the pack. Beta wolves are second-in-command. They help the alphas run the pack.

Deltas guard their pack's **territory**.
Omegas are the lowest rank.

Wolf pack **howls** have many meanings. Some howls call the pack together. Howls can also plan hunts or show pack **unity**.

Wolves bark and growl to warn the pack of danger. They show their teeth when they are angry.

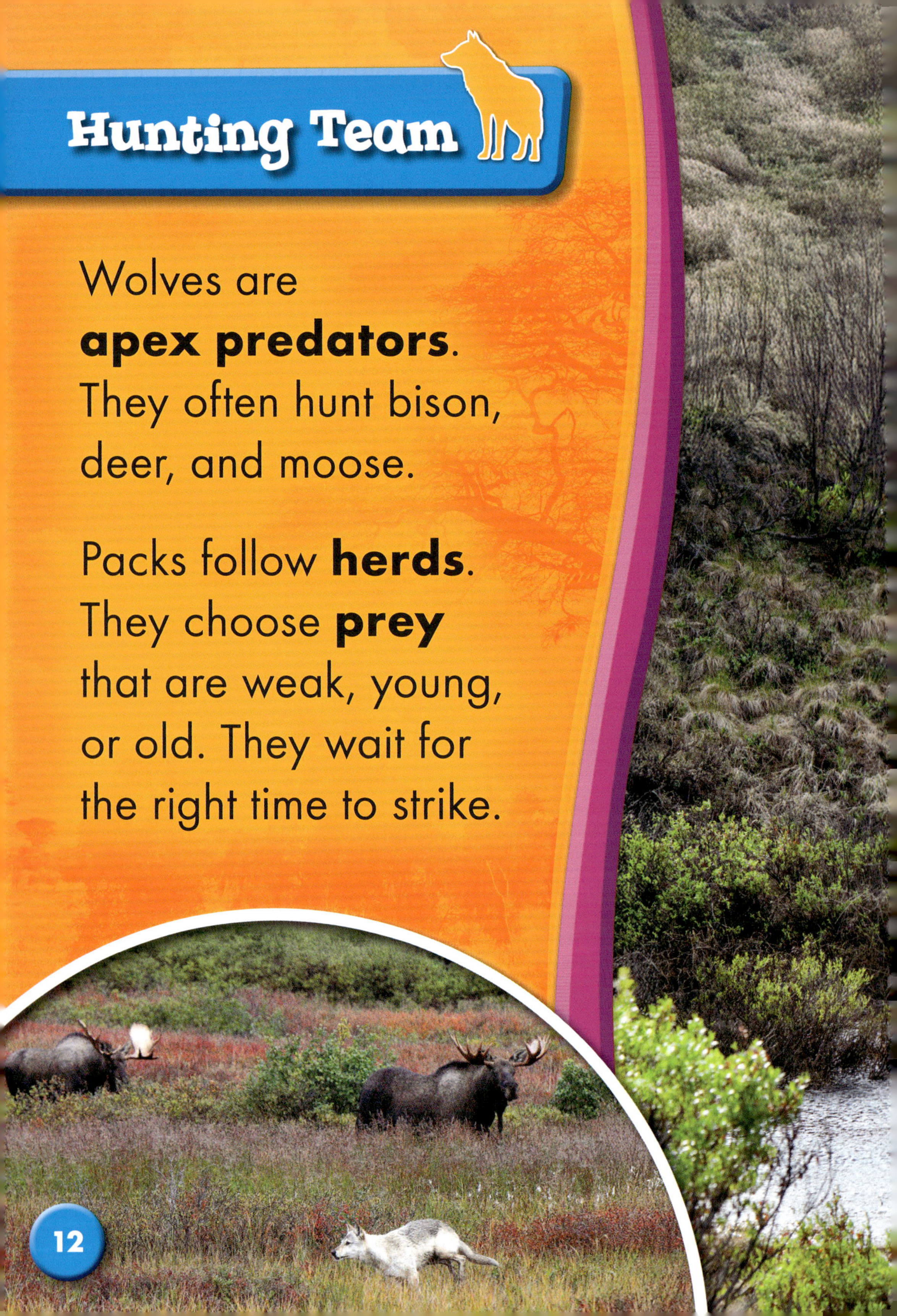

# Hunting Team

Wolves are **apex predators**. They often hunt bison, deer, and moose.

Packs follow **herds**. They choose **prey** that are weak, young, or old. They wait for the right time to strike.

Wolf Diet
bison
deer
moose

Wolf packs hunt as a team. The pack separates one animal from its herd.

Then, the wolves chase the prey until it gets tired. Last, they surround the animal and attack.

follow a herd

separate and chase one animal from the herd

surround the animal and attack

Packs often feed by rank.
The alpha pair eats first.
The beta and other ranks follow.

Sometimes, lower ranked wolves eat ahead of their turn.

# Playful Pups

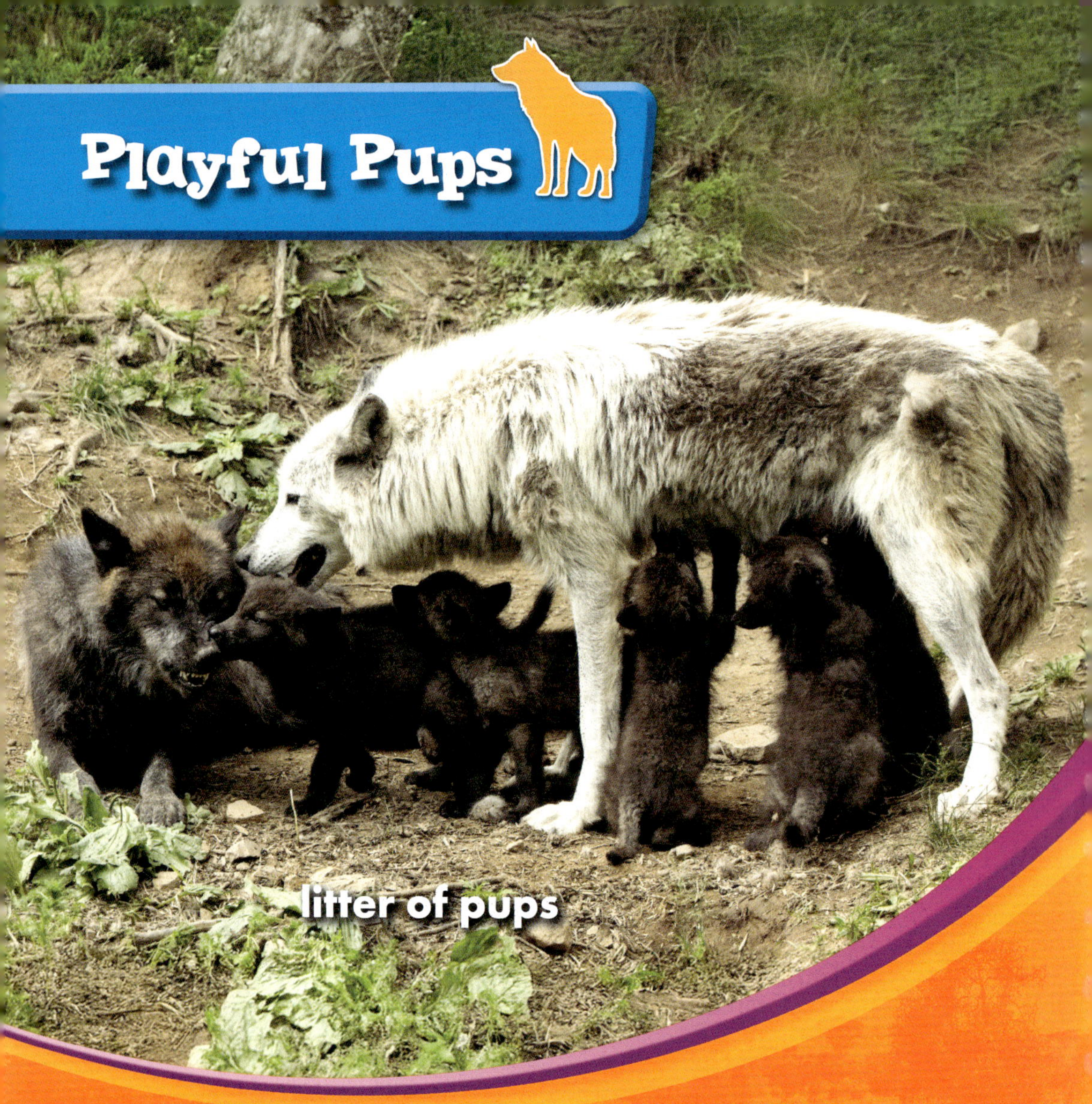

litter of pups

The alpha pair has **pups** once a year. Most **litters** have four to six pups.

The mother and pups stay in **dens**. Pack members bring food to the mother and her pups.

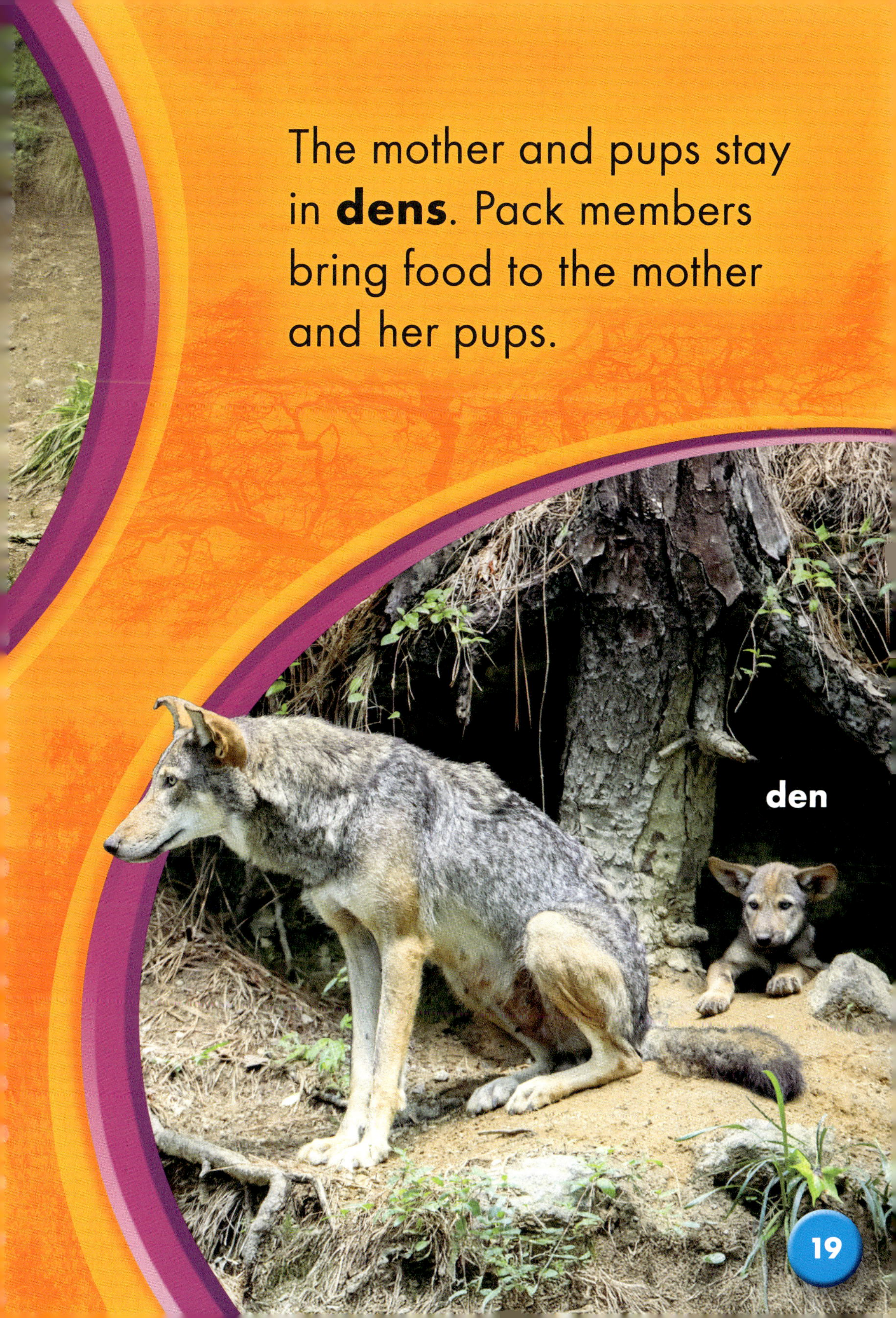

Pack members help watch over and play with the pups. They teach the pups hunting skills as they grow.

Some wolves stay in their birth pack. Others leave and start a new pack of their own!

# Glossary

**alpha pair**–the male and female leaders of a wolf pack

**apex predators**–animals at the top of the food chain that are not preyed upon by other animals

**bonds**–strong attachments

**dens**–sheltered places

**grasslands**–lands covered with grasses and other soft plants with few bushes or trees

**herds**–groups of animals that live and travel together

**howls**–long, loud cries

**litters**–groups of babies that are born at the same time

**offspring**–the young of a male and female pair

**prey**–animals that are hunted by other animals for food

**pups**–baby wolves

**territory**–the land area where an animal lives

**unity**–a feeling of oneness

# To Learn More

## AT THE LIBRARY

Bowman, Chris. *Gray Wolves.* Minneapolis, Minn.: Bellwether Media, 2025.

Bullard, Lisa. *Wolf Packs.* Mendota Heights, Minn.: Focus Readers, 2025.

Salas, Laura Purdie. *Wolf.* Mankato, Minn.: Creative Education and Creative Paperbacks, 2025.

## ON THE WEB

**FACTSURFER**

Factsurfer.com gives you a safe, fun way to find more information.

1. Go to www.factsurfer.com.
2. Enter "wolf packs" into the search box and click 🔍.
3. Select your book cover to see a list of related content.

# Index

Africa, 5
alpha pair, 6, 8, 16, 18
apex predators, 12
Asia, 5
bark, 11
beta, 8, 16
bonds, 8
communication, 11
deltas, 9
dens, 19
Europe, 5
food, 12, 13, 19
forests, 4
grasslands, 4
growl, 11
howls, 10
hunts, 10, 12, 14, 20
litters, 18
mother, 19
mountains, 4
North America, 5
offspring, 6
omegas, 9
packs, 5, 6, 7, 8, 9, 10, 11, 12, 14, 16, 19, 20
prey, 12, 15
pups, 18, 19, 20
range, 5
teeth, 11
territory, 9
wild dogs, 4
working together, 15

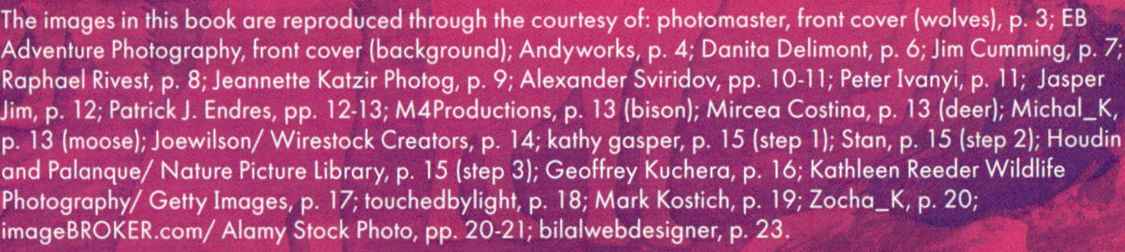

The images in this book are reproduced through the courtesy of: photomaster, front cover (wolves), p. 3; EB Adventure Photography, front cover (background); Andyworks, p. 4; Danita Delimont, p. 6; Jim Cumming, p. 7; Raphael Rivest, p. 8; Jeannette Katzir Photog, p. 9; Alexander Sviridov, pp. 10-11; Peter Ivanyi, p. 11; Jasper Jim, p. 12; Patrick J. Endres, pp. 12-13; M4Productions, p. 13 (bison); Mircea Costina, p. 13 (deer); Michal_K, p. 13 (moose); Joewilson/ Wirestock Creators, p. 14; kathy gasper, p. 15 (step 1); Stan, p. 15 (step 2); Houdin and Palanque/ Nature Picture Library, p. 15 (step 3); Geoffrey Kuchera, p. 16; Kathleen Reeder Wildlife Photography/ Getty Images, p. 17; touchedbylight, p. 18; Mark Kostich, p. 19; Zocha_K, p. 20; imageBROKER.com/ Alamy Stock Photo, pp. 20-21; bilalwebdesigner, p. 23.